# "GO TO BED!"

## CREDITS

*Producer*
  Ron Berry

*Editor*
  Orly Kelly

# What to do
# when your mom or dad says ...

## "GO TO BED!"

By
JOY BERRY

GROLIER ENTERPRISES CORP.

Has your mother or father ever told you to...

Whenever you are told to go to bed, do you wonder. . .

If any of this sounds familiar to you, you are going to **love** this book!

Because it will explain why you need to go to bed and how you can make bedtime something to look forward to.

You are a human being, and human beings need sleep.

Because sleep gives your body a chance to repair itself and to grow. Sleep also allows your body to build up energy.

If you do not get enough sleep, you may become cross and cranky. You may even get sick.

Because disease germs attack a tired person more easily than a rested one.

Thus, it is important that you sleep.

It is up to you and your parents to decide when you should go to bed and how long you should sleep. Here is some information that may help you make your decision:

Research shows that—

- children 6 to 9 years of age need approximately 10 to 11 hours of sleep every night.
- children 10 to 12 years of age need approximately 8 to 9 hours of sleep every night.

Children and parents should keep these needs in mind when they set the hour for bedtime.

Once you and your parents have decided on your bedtime, stick to it.

Do not resist going to bed by stalling.

Do not resist bedtime by whining and nagging.

Stalling, whining, and nagging will only upset your parents and create problems for everyone.

Sleep is not something for you to dread.

Sleep is always the perfect ending to every day.

If you are going to get the most out of going to bed, you'll need to handle it properly. The rest of this book will tell you how.

# APPROACHING BEDTIME

Do not do anything before going to bed that may keep you from sleeping. Avoid things like having upsetting conversations or activities that stimulate you, such as roughhousing.

Do not do anything that might cause you to have nightmares. Avoid things like horror movies, or scary books or stories late at night.

Do not wait until your bedtime to begin getting ready for bed. About 30 minutes before bedtime, stop what you are doing and put your things away. Cleaning up after yourself should not take more than 15 minutes. If it is going to take longer, stop whatever you're doing sooner. Give yourself enough time to do the job correctly. The remaining 15 minutes may be spent getting yourself and your room ready for sleeping.

# BEFORE YOU GET INTO BED

**Prepare yourself** for bed by doing these four things:

1. Take a hot bath or shower. While you are doing this, relax and concentrate on the fact that you are getting ready for bed. (If you choose to take your bath or shower in the morning, it's OK for you to skip doing it again at nighttime.)

2. Brush your hair (if necessary) and clean your teeth.

3. Go to the bathroom.

4. Put on nightclothes that are right for the temperature of your room. If your room is hot, wear something cool. On a very hot night, you may want to sleep under just a sheet.

If your room is cold, wear something warm. Your nightclothes should fit loosely.

Avoid wearing any jewelry that could scratch or choke you.

Avoid going to bed with anything in your mouth that you could choke on, such as gum or candy.

BUT DON'T PUT SNAILS IN YOUR MOUTH.

Avoid drinking anything right before going to bed so you won't have to urinate during the night. You might want to put a glass of water by your bed in case you get thirsty during the night. Be sure to put the glass in a place where you won't accidentally knock it over.

After you have prepared yourself, **prepare your room** by doing these six things:

1. Look all around your bedroom to see that it is safe. Make sure there is nothing in it that could harm you.

2. Check your windows. If you are afraid that something can get into your room from the outside, lock your windows.

   If you prefer to have fresh air come into your room, you can buy a metal stop for your window frame which allows the window to be opened only a certain number of inches.

Checking your room and windows will help you feel safe and should help you avoid having nightmares.

3. Do whatever you can to make sure you will not be too hot or too cold while you are sleeping. If it is possible to control the temperature in your room, keep it under 66° F. at night.

You may want to put an extra folded blanket at the foot of your bed in case you might need it for warmth in the middle of the night.

4. Set your alarm clock, or have someone else agree to wake you at a specific time, so that you will not worry about getting up late.

5. If you are like many children, you may be afraid of the dark. This is because the darkness prevents you from seeing whether anything dangerous is near you. If this is true, turn on a night light.

6. Close your bedroom door enough to shut out the sounds and movements that could disturb your sleep.

If you feel trapped with the door completely closed, do one of these two things:

- leave the door slightly open, or
- ask your parents to open the door all the way once you have gone to sleep.

Here again is a list of the things you need to do to get ready for bed:

**To prepare yourself —**

1. Take a hot bath or shower.
2. Brush your hair and clean your teeth.
3. Go to the bathroom.
4. Put on your nightclothes.

**To prepare your room —**

1. Check your room.
2. Check your windows.
3. Check the room temperature.
4. Set your alarm.
5. Turn on a night light.
6. Close the bedroom door.

Once you have done these things, you are ready
to get into bed.

## AFTER YOU ARE IN BED

Prepare your mind for sleep.

Bedtime is not the time to think about things in your life that are troubling you. Worrying can keep you awake. If you do not rest, you will not have enough energy to work at solving your problems.

Just remember that problems are usually easier to face when you have "slept on them" for a night. They are also easier to solve when you are rested.

If negative thoughts are controlling your mind, replace them with positive ones. Begin by recalling a pleasant experience, or by thinking about something pleasant that is going to happen in the future.

Once you have replaced your negative thoughts with positive ones, try to clear your mind. Let yourself feel and enjoy the wonderful rest that your mind and body are about to experience.

Once your mind is ready for sleep, prepare your body by relaxing. One way to relax your body is to lie flat on your back, stretch your legs out, place your feet slightly apart, put your arms down at your sides, turn the palms of your hands up, and close your eyes.

While you are in this position, mentally count to 10. With each count, tense your body a little more so that by the time you reach 10, your body is completely tightened from head to toe.

After you have completely tensed your body,
begin to count to 10 again. This time, relax more
and more with each count. By the time you reach
the number 10, you should be completely relaxed.

While you are in this relaxed position, think to yourself, "My toes are completely relaxed." As you think this, relax your toes. Next, think to yourself, "My feet are completely relaxed," and relax your feet. Do the same for your legs. Then do the same thing to every part of your body. Once you are totally relaxed, sleep will take over your mind and body.

It is best for you to sleep on your back or your side. It is not good for you to sleep on your stomach.

CORRECT

CORRECT

INCORRECT

**CORRECT**

**iNCORRECT**

If you use a pillow, be sure that it is under your neck, not your head. Your head should not be tilted up or down. Your mattress should be as firm as possible so that it can support your body properly.

# WHILE YOU ARE SLEEPING

If you should have a nightmare, do one of these four things:

1. Call out for help.

2. Go to get help.

3. Help yourself by turning the lights on. Look around your room. See for yourself that you are not in danger.

4. Start thinking about positive things. Remember, you can think only so many thoughts at a time. If you are thinking pleasant thoughts, you can't be thinking scary thoughts; if you are dreaming pleasant dreams, you can't be having nightmares.

You should avoid getting into bed with your parents or anyone else. It is OK to do this once in awhile, but don't make it a habit. You need to learn to sleep alone.

Try to remember what your nightmare was about. Talk it over with someone who might be able to help you understand it. Do this at a time when the person can really listen to you. The middle of the night is not always a good time for this. The other person might be too sleepy to listen.

**THE END** of hating bedtime and having sleepless nights.